The Joy of Living

BY

THOMAS N. STANTON

TABLE OF CONTENTS

Introduction

A young lady named Sarah was struggling with depression. She had been dealing with it for a long time and it seemed to be taking its toll on her. She was feeling incredibly lonely and isolated, and she was struggling to cope with everyday life.

One day, Sarah decided to try something new. She went out and bought a journal and started to write down her thoughts and feelings. As she wrote, she found herself slowly beginning to open up and express her emotions. She started to realize that she was not alone and that there were people who could understand and support her.

Sarah slowly started to make small steps towards recovery. She connected with friends and family and started to build a support network around her. She started to take small steps out of her comfort zone and do things that made her feel alive and excited.

As time went on, Sarah's depression slowly started to lift. She started to experience the joy of living and feel a sense of lasting happiness. She found that she was able to cope with life's challenges and face them with a newfound strength and courage.

Sarah eventually realized that she had the power to take control of her life and create a life that she was proud of. She was no longer living in depression and instead was able to experience the joy of living.

Sarah's story is a reminder to us all that with the right support and willingness to take brave steps forward, it is possible to overcome depression and experience lasting happiness.

Welcome to the wonderful world of lasting happiness! In The Joy of Living: A Guide to Lasting Happiness, we will explore the depths of true, lasting joy and how to bring it into your life.

This book was written with the hope of helping readers create a life of lasting joy, satisfaction, and fulfillment. It is a guide to living a life that is free of anxiety, sadness, and stress. It is a journey of self-discovery and personal growth that will lead you to a life of true inner peace.

We will explore the various aspects of living a life of lasting joy and happiness. We will discuss the different approaches to achieving lasting happiness, such as mindfulness, positive thinking, and self-care. We will also look at the science behind positive emotions and how to cultivate them. We will also explore the power of our thoughts and how to use them to create positive change in our lives.

In addition, we will look at the importance of relationships and how to develop and maintain meaningful connections with others. We will discuss the benefits of having a spiritual practice and how it can lead to a more fulfilling life. We will also explore the power of gratitude and how it can lead to greater joy and contentment.

Finally, we will examine the power of our subconscious minds and how we can use it to create lasting joy and happiness in our lives. We will look at ways to break free from the negative patterns that often prevent us from living our best lives. We will discuss how to change our inner dialogue and create a life that is free from self-doubt and negative beliefs.

By the end of this book, you will have the tools and insights needed to create a life of lasting joy and happiness. You will have the knowledge and understanding necessary to create positive changes in your life and live with more joy and contentment. So, let us begin our journey together and explore the wonderful path to lasting happiness.

Welcome to The Joy of Living: A Guide to Lasting Happiness!

Part I: Cultivating Happiness

Happiness is often described as a feeling of contentment, joy, and satisfaction. It is an emotion that can range from deep, lasting contentment to fleeting moments of joy. It is an emotion that many of us strive for, and it is a feeling that can bring us a sense of purpose and satisfaction.

Happiness can come from a variety of sources. It can come from within ourselves, from our relationships, or from our environment. It can come from our career, our hobbies, our spiritual practice, or any other area of our life. It can also come from a combination of these sources. Whatever the source, true happiness is something that we all strive to achieve.

When we are feeling happy, we tend to be more compassionate, kind, and generous. We are more likely to be patient with others and to be open to learning and growth. We can also be more creative, better problem solvers, and more apt to take risks and try new things. This combination of positive effects can help us to achieve our goals and to make a difference in the world.

Happiness isn't just a feeling, it can also be a choice. We can choose to focus on the positive things in our lives, to practice gratitude and self-care, to laugh and to be kind to ourselves and to others. We can choose to take time for ourselves, to spend time outdoors, to nurture relationships, and to focus on our goals. Through these choices, we can create a life that is full of joy and contentment.

Happiness is something that we all strive for and something that can bring us a sense of purpose and satisfaction. It is a feeling that can be found in the small moments, in the big moments, and in the everyday moments. True happiness is something that can be cultivated, and it is a choice that we can make every day.

Chapter 1: Finding Meaning in Life

Finding meaning in life is a common challenge for many people. Some might feel that life has no purpose, while others may feel overwhelmed by the responsibility of finding a sense of purpose. Whatever the case, it's important to remember that everyone's life has meaning and purpose.

The first step to finding meaning in life is to identify what's important to you. This can be done by reflecting on your values and goals in life. What do you want to achieve in life? What makes you feel good? What do you want to learn? Once you've identified these things, it's time to take action.

Start small and take one step at a time. This can be as simple as making a list of things you want to do and setting aside time to do them. If you want to learn a new skill, find a class or program that can help you do so. If you want to travel, research your options. Making a plan and taking action is the best way to move closer to achieving your goals.

Surround yourself with people who understand and share your values. Being around like-minded people can help you stay motivated and focused on achieving your goals. Find a mentor who is successful in a field that you're passionate about, and use them as a source of guidance and support.

Take some time each day to do something that makes you feel good. This could be meditating, exercising, or reading a book. Taking time for yourself can help you feel more energized and motivated.

Finally, remember to be kind to yourself. Life is unpredictable, and it's easy to get overwhelmed by the unexpected. Don't be too hard on yourself if things don't go as planned. Accept that things are out of your control, and use it as an opportunity to learn and grow.

Finding meaning in life is a process, and it starts with taking the time to identify what's important to you. Once you know what you want, take action and surround yourself with people who will support you. Don't forget to take care of yourself and be kind to yourself along the way. With dedication and effort, you can find meaning and purpose in life.

Your life has meaning and purpose, you just have to find it.

30 steps you can take to find meaning in life:

1. Take time for yourself: Make sure to take time for yourself each day to do something that brings you joy and allows you to relax. This will help you to gain clarity and perspective.

2. Find your passion: Find something you are truly passionate about and make it an integral part of your life. It can be a hobby, sport, or something creative.

3. **Pursue your goals**: Set short-term and long-term goals that are attainable and make sure to take the steps necessary to achieve them.

4. **Connect with nature**: Spend time in nature and appreciate the beauty and complexity of the world around you.

5. **Reconnect with old friends**: Reconnecting with old friends who you have lost touch with.

6. **Make new friends**: Make new friends and get to know different people to broaden your understanding of the world.

7. **Volunteer**: Give back to the community by volunteering for a cause that you are passionate about.

8. **Exercise**: Exercise regularly to maintain your physical health and mental clarity.

9. **Read**: Read books, articles, and magazines that help you learn and grow.

10. **Write**: Write down your thoughts, ideas, and feelings to gain clarity and insight into your life.

11. **Meditate**: Take time every day to practice meditation to help clear your mind and gain focus.

12. **Set boundaries**: Set boundaries in your relationships to protect your emotional and mental health.

13. Get organized: Get organized and declutter your life to make sure that you are focused on the things that matter most.

14. Spend time with family: Spend quality time with your family to strengthen your connections and appreciate the people closest to you.

15. Help others: Take the time to help others and make a positive difference in their lives.

16. Express gratitude: Express gratitude for the people and experiences in your life to appreciate them more deeply.

17. Challenge yourself: Push yourself out of your comfort zone and challenge yourself to reach your full potential.

18. Learn something new: Take the time to learn something new to broaden your knowledge and understanding.

19. Get creative: Get creative and explore different mediums to express yourself and explore new interests.

20. Take risks: Take risks and be open to new experiences to make your life more interesting and dynamic.

21. Travel: Take the time to travel and explore the world to gain a new perspective on life.

22. Live with intention: Live with intention and make conscious decisions that will move you closer to your goals.

23. Embrace change: Embrace change and be open to the possibilities that come with it.

24. Find balance: Find balance in your relationships, work, and hobbies to create a more harmonious life.

25. Live in the present: Live in the present moment and appreciate the beauty of life.

26. Let go of grudges: Let go of grudges and forgive yourself and others to move on from the past.

27. Spend time alone: Spend time alone to reflect on your life and gain clarity.

28. Follow your instincts: Follow your instincts and trust your gut to make the right decisions.

29. Take care of yourself: Take care of yourself by getting enough sleep, eating well, and exercising regularly.

30. Believe in yourself: Believe in yourself and your abilities to achieve your goals and find meaning in life.

The ultimate goal of life is to seek meaning and purpose, and it is up to each individual to decide what that means for them. For some, it may be a career, a religion, or a cause, while others may find meaning in relationships, hobbies, or simply enjoying the moments of life. There is no one-size-fits-all answer to finding meaning in life, and everyone must discover what works for them.

One of the most important ways to find meaning in life is to focus on the present and live in the moment. Cultivating a sense of gratitude and appreciation for what you have can help you to appreciate life more and find joy in the little things. Additionally, it is important to be kind and generous to others, as acts of kindness can make a big difference in the lives of those around you and make you feel more connected to the world.

Remember, it is important to stay motivated and take risks. Life is full of uncertainties, and taking risks can help you to explore new possibilities and make changes that can lead to a more meaningful existence. Taking risks can also help you to develop a greater sense of self-worth and build confidence in your ability to make a positive difference in the world.

The search for meaning in life is a lifelong journey, and there is no one-size-fits-all answer. Everyone must find what works for them and make the most of the time they have. Remember that life is a journey and not a destination, and that every day is an opportunity to make it a more meaningful experience.

No matter who you are or where you are in life, it is possible to find meaning and purpose. With dedication and an open mind, you can make the most of your life and find a more meaningful existence.

Finding meaning in life is an individual journey that must be undertaken by each person. It is important to stay in the present, practice kindness and generosity, and take risks to explore new possibilities. Everyone must find what works for them and make the most of the time they have. With dedication and an open mind, everyone can make the most of their life and find a more meaningful existence.

Chapter 2: Developing Positive Habits

What are Positive Habits?

Positive habits are habits that lead to a person's overall wellbeing. They are habits that are beneficial to both physical and mental health, and lead to a more successful, productive, and happier life.

Good habits can be developed through practice and dedication. This means that, with consistent effort, a person can develop and maintain habits that will positively affect their everyday life. Examples of positive habits include exercising regularly, eating a balanced diet, developing a good sleep routine, being organized, setting goals, being mindful of others, practicing gratitude, and taking time for yourself.

In terms of physical health, regular exercise helps to reduce the risk of heart disease, stroke, and diabetes, as well as promote weight management. Eating a balanced diet helps to ensure that the body gets the nutrients it needs to function properly and can help prevent illnesses and disease. Additionally, having a good sleep routine helps to reduce stress and improve overall physical health.

In terms of mental health, positive habits can help to reduce stress, improve productivity, and develop positive relationships. Setting goals and being organized can help to stay on track with daily tasks and increase productivity. Being mindful of others promotes better relationships and can help to develop trust and understanding. Practicing gratitude helps to shift focus away from negative thoughts and can help to increase happiness. Additionally, taking time for yourself can help to reduce stress and improve overall wellbeing.

Overall, positive habits are beneficial for both physical and mental health. With consistent practice and dedication, these habits can lead to improved overall wellbeing and a healthier, happier life.

Developing positive habits is essential for achieving success in every area of life. Habits are the repetitive behaviors that we do every day. They are the foundation of our character and the way we interact with the world. By developing good habits, we can create a better, more fulfilling life for ourselves.

Positive habits can help us to reach our goals, manage stress, and improve our overall wellbeing. They involve the development of skills and behaviors that are beneficial to our physical and mental health. Examples of positive habits include eating healthy, exercising regularly, getting enough sleep, and focusing on our mental health. Additionally, positive habits can involve developing relationships, being kind to others, and setting realistic goals.

Developing positive habits is a lifelong process that requires dedication and a commitment to making changes. It's important to be aware of our current habits and identify areas where we need to make changes. We can then create a plan for developing new habits, setting goals, and tracking our progress.

By consistently practicing positive habits, we can build a strong foundation for a successful and fulfilling life. Developing positive habits can help us to become more productive, successful, and content with our lives. Furthermore, by understanding our current habits and making positive changes, we can create a healthier and more fulfilling lifestyle.

It is important to note that, developing positive habits is essential for creating a successful and fulfilling life. It involves the development of beneficial habits that can help us reach our goals and improve our wellbeing. Additionally, by setting goals, tracking our progress, and being consistent in our efforts, we can create a strong foundation for a successful and fulfilling life.

Developing positive habits is essential for achieving success in every area of life. It can help us to reach our goals, manage stress, and improve our overall wellbeing. Furthermore, by understanding our current habits and making positive changes, we can create a healthier and more fulfilling lifestyle.

So start today, and begin building your positive habits for a successful and fulfilling life.

Here are 20 new lifestyle habits you can develop:

1. **Wake up early**: Waking up earlier allows you to start your day with more energy and a better focus on what needs to be done.
2. **Exercise regularly**: Regular exercise has numerous benefits for both your physical and mental health.
3. **Eat healthy**: Eating healthy foods is important for maintaining your energy levels and staying healthy.
4. **Drink plenty of water**: Staying hydrated can help boost energy and aid in digestion.
5. **Practice mindfulness**: Practicing mindfulness can help reduce stress and aid in calming the mind.
6. **Get enough sleep**: Getting enough sleep helps the body to rest and recharge so that it can perform better during the day.
7. **Reduce screen time**: Reducing the amount of time spent on screens can help reduce eye strain and improve mental health.
8. **Take breaks**: Taking regular breaks throughout the day can help to reduce stress and improve focus.
9. **Read books**: Reading books helps to expand your knowledge and can also be a great way to relax.
10. **Get organized**: Getting organized can help to reduce stress and make it easier to accomplish tasks.
11. **Take time for yourself**: Taking time for yourself can help to reduce stress and give you time to relax and reflect.

12. Develop a hobby: Developing a hobby can help to give you something to look forward to and can also help to reduce stress.
13. Spend time with friends and family: Spending time with friends and family can help to reduce stress and give you a sense of connection.
14. Learn a new skill: Learning a new skill can be a great way to challenge yourself and keep your mind active.
15. Take up a sport: Taking up a sport can help to keep you active and can also be a great way to socialize.
16. Practice self-care: Taking care of yourself is important for your physical and mental health.
17. Get out in nature: Spending time in nature can help to reduce stress and can also improve your mood.
18. Unplug from technology: Taking a break from technology can help to reduce stress and give you more time to focus on other things.
19. Learn to manage stress: Learning how to manage stress is important for maintaining your mental health and wellbeing.
20. Develop a positive attitude: Having a positive attitude can help to reduce stress and make it easier to deal with difficult situations.

We are all aware that creating new habits may be challenging, and maintaining them can be even more challenging. Here are some strategies for creating a reliable plan for forming a new habit or hobby.

1. **Identify Your Goal**: First and foremost, you must identify the habit you would like to develop. It should be a specific and achievable goal. For example, if your goal is to become more organized, decide on one specific task that you can do to help reach that goal.

2. **Make a Plan**: Once you have identified your goal, you need to create a plan of action. Make a list of all the steps that you need to take in order to reach your goal. For example, if you want to become more organized, break it down into smaller, manageable tasks such as creating a to-do list, setting aside time each day to complete tasks, and using a planner or calendar to keep track of your progress.

3. **Track Your Progress**: Once you have made a plan, you need to track your progress and hold yourself accountable. Start by setting small, achievable goals and then reward yourself when you reach them. This will help keep you motivated and on track.

4. **Establish a Routine**: Establishing a routine is key to developing a new habit. Start by scheduling specific times to work on your goal and try to stick to it as much as possible. This will help you create a consistent pattern of behavior and will make it easier to stay on track.

5. **Seek Support**: Last but not least, don't be afraid to seek help and support from your friends and family. Having someone to hold you accountable and to provide encouragement can make a world of difference.

Developing a new habit can be a challenging process but with commitment and dedication, it can be done. Remember to take it one step at a time and focus on small, achievable goals. With time and effort, you will be able to successfully develop a new habit.

Chapter 3: Cultivating Gratitude

What is Gratitude?

Gratitude is an emotion that we can all benefit from feeling more often. It is the feeling of appreciation for the good things in our lives, both big and small. When we express gratitude, it helps us to recognize what we have and savor the positive moments in our lives. It can help to improve our mental and physical health, as well as our relationships.

Gratitude can be expressed in various ways. We can express our gratitude through words, gestures, and even through our actions. We can thank someone for something they did, write a thank-you note, or simply tell someone how much we appreciate them. We can also express gratitude to ourselves, by recognizing our own strengths, successes, and accomplishments.

Expressing gratitude is a powerful way to cultivate positive emotions and relationships. It can help to reduce stress and increase happiness. Research shows that people who regularly express gratitude have better physical and mental health, are more optimistic and resilient, and have better relationships.

Gratitude can also motivate us to take action and make positive changes in our lives. When we appreciate the good things in our lives, it can help us to focus on the present moment and make the most of our lives. We can use gratitude as a way to prioritize our goals, focus on our strengths and aspirations, and find meaning and purpose in our lives.

Gratitude can be a habit, and the more we practice it, the easier it becomes. We can start by simply taking a moment each day to appreciate the good things in our lives. We can practice gratitude by writing down three things we are grateful for each day, or by meditating on the things we are thankful for. We can also practice expressing gratitude to others by saying thank you, writing a thank-you note, or simply showing appreciation.

Gratitude is an emotion that can help us to live more fully and appreciate the good things in life. By expressing gratitude, we can increase our happiness, reduce stress, and strengthen our relationships. Gratitude can also motivate us to take positive action and make positive changes in our lives. By making gratitude a habit, we can learn to appreciate the present and make the most of our lives.

Gratitude is an emotion that can help us to live more fully and appreciate the good things in life. By expressing gratitude, we can increase our happiness, reduce stress, and strengthen our relationships. Gratitude can also motivate us to take positive action and make positive changes in our lives. By making gratitude a habit, we can learn to appreciate the present and make the most of our lives.

Being grateful is a state of appreciation and thankfulness for the good things in life. It is an acknowledgement of the goodness that exists in our lives and the world around us. Gratitude is a feeling of thankfulness for the people, things, and experiences that have enriched our lives.

Gratitude can be expressed in many different ways, from simply saying "thank you" to showing kindness to others. It is important to recognize and express our gratefulness for the good things in life. When we express our gratitude, we open ourselves up to more positive energy and experiences.

Gratitude can also help us to shift our perspective and become more aware of the beauty and abundance in our lives. It can help us to appreciate the little things, cultivate a sense of contentment, and stay focused on the positives. Expressing our gratitude can help us to stay present and mindful in the moment, and can also increase our feelings of joy and happiness.

Finally, gratitude can help us to foster deeper connections with others. By expressing our appreciation for the people, things, and experiences that bring us joy, we create stronger relationships and a sense of community.

Grateful living can bring us closer to our true selves and the people we love. It is a powerful and transformative practice that can help us to become more mindful and connected to the world around us.

Being grateful is a choice and a practice, and it can open up a world of abundance and joy. The more we express our appreciation and thankfulness for the good things in life, the more we will be able to experience the joy of living.

Practical Methods of Expressing Gratitude

Expressing gratitude is a powerful way to show appreciation and build meaningful relationships with others. It can be done in a variety of ways and is an important part of life. Here are some tips on how to express gratitude:

1. Acknowledge the effort: Acknowledge the effort that someone has put in to help you or make a difference in your life. This could be in the form of a thank you note, a phone call, or even a simple "thank you" when you see them.

2. Offer a Gift: Offering a gift to show your appreciation is a great way to express gratitude. It doesn't need to be expensive, something small but meaningful will do.

3. Show Appreciation in Person: Showing appreciation in person is much more meaningful than a thank you note or phone call. Make sure to give the person your full attention and express your gratitude with sincerity.

4. Make it Personal: Make your “thank you” more personal by expressing what you appreciate about the person or the situation. This could be something specific that they did or a trait that they have.

5. Express Gratitude Every Day: Expressing gratitude doesn’t have to be a one-time thing. Find ways to show appreciation every day. This could be through words, actions, or even just a smile.

Expressing gratitude is an important part of life and can make a huge difference in relationships. Showing appreciation for the people in your life can help you build meaningful connections and make them feel valued.

Part II: Building Resilience

Resilience is the ability to adapt to, or cope with, difficult situations, changes or challenges. It is the capacity to recover quickly from difficulties or to adjust easily to changing circumstances. Resilience is an important life skill that can help people cope with stress, hardships, and traumatic events.

Resilience is a key factor in managing change and adversity. People with resilience are better able to cope with difficult situations, and bounce back from failures and setbacks. They are more able to handle difficult emotions, such as fear, anger, and sadness, and to remain hopeful and optimistic in the face of adversity. Resilience also helps people to build stronger relationships and to better manage work and family responsibilities.

Resilience is not a fixed trait. It is a skill that can be developed and strengthened over time with practice. There are many strategies and techniques that can help to increase resilience, such as:

- Developing positive thinking skills
- Practicing self-care
- Setting realistic goals

- Developing problem-solving skills
- Connecting with a supportive network
- Developing a sense of purpose
- Learning to manage stress
- Taking time for relaxation
- Practicing gratitude
- Practicing relaxation techniques
- Getting enough sleep
- Exercise and physical activity
- Developing a positive attitude
- Working on communication skills
- Practicing mindfulness

Practicing these strategies can help to increase your resilience and improve your ability to cope with difficult times. It is important to remember that resilience is not a one-time event. It is a process of learning and adapting that requires ongoing effort and practice.

For the purpose of this book, we shall be discussing the topics: Managing Stress, Overcoming Adversity and Developing Self-Compassion as means of Developing Resilience.

Chapter 4: Managing Stress

Stress is an emotional and physical strain caused by an individual's response to pressure from their environment. It can be triggered by a variety of factors, such as work, school, relationships, or even everyday events. While it's true that everyone experiences stress to some extent, it's important to understand how it affects your body and how to manage it effectively.

When it comes to the physical effects of stress, it's important to be aware of the changes that can occur. For example, during a stressful situation, the body releases hormones such as cortisol and adrenaline, which can affect heart rate, blood pressure, and digestion. Stress can also cause headaches, muscle tension, and fatigue. Long-term stress can result in more serious health issues such as high blood pressure, heart disease, and depression.

In order to cope with stress, it's important to take a proactive approach. One way to do this is to practice relaxation techniques such as deep breathing and progressive muscle relaxation. Exercise can also be an effective way to reduce stress, as it can help to release endorphins, which are hormones that make you feel good. Additionally, eating a healthy diet, getting enough sleep, and participating in leisure activities can also help to reduce stress.

It's important to recognize when stress is becoming too much and to seek professional help if needed. Talking to a counselor or therapist can be beneficial in helping you to identify and address the underlying causes of your stress. They can also provide strategies to help you better manage your stress and develop healthy coping skills.

Stress can be an unavoidable part of life, but it's important to be aware of the physical and emotional effects that it can have. Taking a proactive approach, such as practicing relaxation techniques, exercising, and seeking professional help, can help you to better manage your stress and lead a healthier, more balanced life.

Kinds of stress

Stress is a normal and natural part of life. It can be beneficial when it motivates us to take action or be more productive. However, too much stress can have a negative impact on our mental and physical health. There are several types of stress, each with its own unique characteristics and effects.

1. **Acute Stress**: Acute stress is a short-term response to an immediate threat or challenge. It typically occurs when we are faced with a difficult situation that requires a quick response. Acute stress can help

us stay focused and alert, but it can also lead to anxiety and other physical symptoms if it is prolonged.

2. **Chronic Stress**: Chronic stress is a long-term response to a sustained or repeated threat or challenge. It is often caused by ongoing issues such as a demanding job, financial problems, or relationship difficulties. Chronic stress can lead to mental health issues such as depression and anxiety, as well as physical symptoms such as headaches and digestive problems.
3. **Episodic Acute Stress**: Episodic acute stress is a pattern of acute stress that occurs on a regular basis. It is often caused by a series of recurring events or situations, such as an unpredictable work schedule or frequent deadlines. Episodic acute stress can lead to mental and physical health issues if it is not managed properly.
4. **Post-Traumatic Stress Disorder**: Post-traumatic stress disorder (PTSD) is an anxiety disorder that occurs after a traumatic event. Symptoms of PTSD include flashbacks, nightmares, excessive worry, and difficulty sleeping. PTSD can have a significant impact on a person’s life, and professional help is often necessary for recovery.

Stress can be beneficial in some situations, but too much stress can have serious consequences for our mental and physical health. It is important to recognize the different types of stress and to learn how to manage them in order to avoid long-term health problems.

If you are feeling overwhelmed or stressed, it is important to reach out for help. Talk to a friend or family member, or seek professional help if necessary. Taking care of your mental and physical health is essential for living a happy and healthy life.

Effects of Stress on the Human health

Stress is a normal reaction to the pressures of everyday life. It can be beneficial in helping people stay focused, motivated, and alert. But when it becomes excessive, it can have a negative effect on the body.

Stress can affect the body in a variety of ways. It can cause physical symptoms, such as headaches, chest pain, rapid heartbeat, stomach upset, and weakened immune system. It can also cause mental symptoms, such as irritability, restlessness, difficulty concentrating, and feelings of anxiety and depression.

Chronic stress can lead to more serious health problems, such as heart disease, high blood pressure, obesity, diabetes, depression, and even cancer. Stress can also lead to behaviors that can be harmful, such as smoking, drinking too much alcohol, and drug abuse.

One of the most serious effects of stress is on the brain. Stress hormones, such as cortisol, can cause changes in the brain that affect how people think and behave. It can affect the way people remember things and make decisions.

Stress can also cause changes in the brain that can lead to mental health problems, such as anxiety and depression. Stress can also make existing mental health conditions worse.

The best way to cope with stress is to learn how to manage it. This includes getting enough sleep, eating healthy, exercising, taking time for yourself, and talking to someone about your worries. Learning how to relax and manage your stress can help you stay healthy and prevent the negative effects of stress on your body.

Stress has a significant impact on human health. It can cause physical, mental, and emotional symptoms, and can lead to more serious health conditions. Learning how to manage stress can help you stay healthy and prevent the negative effects of stress on your body.

10 ways to effectively manage Stress

1. **Exercise**: Regular physical activity can help reduce stress and improve your overall wellbeing. Exercise releases endorphins which can help to reduce stress and make you feel happier.

2. **Breathe**: Deep breathing exercises can help you to relax and reduce stress. Taking a few minutes to focus on your breathing can help to calm your mind and body.

3. **Talk to someone**: Talking to a friend, family member, therapist or counsellor can help you to process your feelings and find ways to manage your stress.

4. **Get enough sleep**: Lack of sleep can increase stress levels, so make sure you are getting enough rest.

5. **Eat healthily**: Eating a balanced diet can help to keep your energy levels up, which can help to reduce stress.

6. **Take breaks**: Taking regular breaks throughout the day can help to reduce stress. Even a few minutes of relaxation can make a difference.

7. **Learn relaxation techniques**: Relaxation techniques such as yoga, meditation or mindfulness can help to reduce stress.

8. **Stay organised**: Keeping on top of your tasks can help to reduce stress. Make to-do lists, plan ahead and set yourself realistic goals.

9. **Avoid unhealthy coping mechanisms**: Unhealthy coping mechanisms such as smoking, drinking or overeating can make stress worse in the long-term.

10. **Say no**: Taking on too much can be overwhelming and lead to increased stress levels. It's important to know your limits and be able to say no when needed.

Benefits of Living a Stress-free life

Living a stress-free life can bring many benefits to a person's life. Stress can lead to a range of physical, mental and emotional issues, so reducing stress can make a person feel happier and healthier.

One of the main benefits of living a stress-free life is improved physical health. Stress can cause physical symptoms such as headaches, muscle tension, stomach problems, fatigue, and skin problems. By reducing stress, these physical problems can be alleviated. Additionally, living a stress-free life can reduce the risk of high blood pressure and heart disease.

Living a stress-free life can also benefit mental health. Stress can lead to mental health issues such as depression, anxiety, and insomnia. Reducing stress can help to improve focus and concentration, allowing a person to be more productive and creative.

Finally, living a stress-free life can benefit emotional health. Stress can make people feel overwhelmed, anxious, and irritable. When stress is reduced, a person can feel more relaxed and happier. This can lead to improved relationships with family and friends, as well as better performance in work or school.

Overall, living a stress-free life can bring many positive physical, mental and emotional benefits. Reducing stress can help a person to live a happier and healthier life.

Chapter 5: Overcoming Adversity

Adversity is a part of life. It is an inevitable part of the human experience, and it can take many forms. It can be the loss of a job, the death of a loved one, a health crisis, a financial setback, or anything else that disrupts our lives. The reality is that adversity is not only unavoidable but is also essential to our growth and development.

Adversity can be a source of strength. Difficult times can be an opportunity to learn and grow, to develop resilience and courage, and to become more compassionate and understanding people. Adversity can open our eyes to the world around us, to the beauty and fragility of life, and to the strength of the human spirit. It can also provide us with perspective, allowing us to see how much we have to be thankful for.

Adversity can also be a source of stress, fear, and pain. It can be overwhelming, and it can take time to process and move through it. It is important to acknowledge the reality of this pain, to reach out for support, and to practice self-care. Taking care of our mental and physical health is essential in times of adversity, as it can help us cope and eventually move through it.

Adversity is an unavoidable part of life. It can be a source of strength, growth, and understanding, but it can also be a source of stress, fear, and pain. It is important to acknowledge and accept the reality of adversities in our lives, and to practice self-care and seek support when needed. In the end, adversity can help us develop resilience, courage, and compassion, and can open our eyes to the beauty of life.

No matter how difficult our circumstances may be, there is always hope. Adversity can be difficult to face, but it can also bring us closer to our true selves and to our highest potential.

Life is full of adversities that can take many forms. Adversity can range from small, everyday frustrations to major life-altering events. It is important to recognize that everyone faces adversity in life, and it is how we choose to respond to these difficulties that ultimately matters. Here are some of the common forms of adversity we may face in life:

1. **Financial Adversity**: Financial difficulties can be one of the hardest types of adversity to face. Unexpected bills, job loss, and other financial struggles can create a great deal of stress and worry. It is important to remember that financial hardships are temporary, and that there is always hope of a better financial future.

2. **Health Adversity**: Health issues not only affect our physical well-being, but can also have a major impact on our mental and emotional state. Health adversities can include an illness or injury, chronic disease, or a disability. These types of adversities can be difficult to cope with, but with

the right support, it is possible to manage and even find hope and strength during these tough times.

3. **Family Adversity**: Family can be a great source of support and love, but it can also be a source of adversity. Difficult family dynamics, such as divorce, death, or other painful experiences can be hard to manage. It is important to remember that family adversity is not something to be ashamed of, and that with patience, understanding, and communication, it is possible to work through these challenges.

4. **Career Adversity**: Career adversity can include job loss, a lack of job opportunities, or feeling stuck in a job that doesn't meet your needs. It is important to remember that there is always hope, and that with patience and determination, it is possible to find a career that is fulfilling and rewarding.

No matter the form of adversity we face in life, it is important to remember that we are not alone and that it is possible to find strength and hope during difficult times. Adversity can be hard to manage, but with the right support and resources, it is possible to find a way forward.

Practical ways to overcoming Adversity

1. **Keep Moving Forward**: The key to overcoming adversity is to keep moving forward. It's easy to wallow in your distress and give up, but the only way out of a difficult situation is to keep pushing forward. This can be as simple as taking one small step in the right direction each day.

2. **Change Your Perspective**: When life throws you a curveball, try to look at the situation from a different perspective. Rather than focusing on the negative aspects of a situation, look for the positive. This can help you to better understand the challenge and find a solution.

3. **Connect with Others**: Reaching out to family and friends for support can be a great way to cope with adversity. Sharing your struggles with others can help you to gain perspective and find solutions to your problems.

4. **Practice Self-Care**: Taking care of your body and mind is essential when dealing with adversity. Make sure to get enough rest, eat a balanced diet, exercise, and take time to relax. This will help you to stay strong and find the energy to keep pushing forward.

5. **Seek Professional Help**: Don't be afraid to seek professional help if needed. There are many resources available such as counseling, support groups, and mental health professionals who can help you to cope with adversity and find solutions.

6. **Focus on What You Can Control**: When facing adversity, it's important to focus on what you can control rather than what's out of your control. This will help you to remain positive and take action to move forward.

7. **Find Inspiration**: Look for sources of inspiration and motivation that can help you to stay focused and positive in the face of adversity. This could be anything from books and podcasts to mentors and role models.

8. **Take Time to Reflect**: Sometimes it's important to take a step back and reflect on the situation. This can help you to gain clarity on what's causing the difficulty and how you can move forward.

9. **Set Goals**: Setting goals can help to keep you focused and motivated when facing adversity. Break down big goals into smaller achievable steps, and celebrate each step you take towards achieving your goals.

10. **Don't Give Up**: Last but not least, don't give up. Adversity can be difficult to overcome, but it's important to stay strong and keep pushing forward. You are capable of achieving great things if you don't give up.

Adversity is an unavoidable part of life. Everyone will face some form of adversity throughout their lives, whether it is financial, emotional, physical, or any other type. It is important to remember that facing and overcoming adversity can be a rewarding experience that can help you grow as a person and build resilience.

The first step in overcoming adversity is to recognize that it exists. This means accepting that you will have to face difficult situations and finding the strength and courage to do so. Once you have accepted that adversity exists, it is important to focus on the positives. Instead of dwelling on the difficult situation, try to find the silver lining. This could be taking the opportunity to develop a new skill, or simply learning from the experience.

It is also important to take action. Taking action could mean reaching out for support from friends and family, seeking professional help, or finding resources online. Taking action is a sign of strength and courage, and it is key to overcoming adversity.

Another important step in overcoming adversity is to set realistic goals. It can be tempting to set overly ambitious goals, but setting achievable goals is key to success. Start by setting small, achievable goals that you can work towards. As you progress, you can gradually set bigger goals. This will help you stay motivated and on track.

In addition to setting goals, it is important to practice self-care. Take some time to relax and take care of yourself. This could mean taking a hot bath, reading a book, or even going on a walk. Allowing yourself some time to relax will help you stay focused and motivated.

Also, it is important to remember that adversity is not permanent. You can overcome it with the right frame of mind and the right tools. Keep in mind that there is no single solution to overcoming adversity. It is a process that requires patience and perseverance. With the right attitude and some hard work, you can overcome any obstacle.

Adversity can be difficult to overcome, but it can also be rewarding. It can help you build resilience and learn valuable lessons about life. With the right attitude and some hard work, you can overcome any obstacle. So, don't be afraid to face adversity, and use it as an opportunity to learn and grow.

Five key points to always remember about adversities

1. **Adversity is a normal part of life**: Adversity is something that everyone will face at some point in their life. It is important to remember that adversity is part of the human experience and it is not something to be feared or avoided. Learning how to manage and cope with adversity can help you to become a stronger and more resilient person.

2. **You are not alone**: It is easy to feel isolated and alone when facing difficult circumstances. It is important to remember that you are not alone in your struggles and that there are people who are willing to support and help you. Whether it is family, friends, professionals or even online support groups, having a support system can be invaluable when dealing with adversity.

3. **Look for the lesson**: Adversity can often provide valuable lessons. It can teach you about yourself, your values and what is important to you. It can also give you the opportunity to grow and learn from your experience.

4. **Take things one step at a time**: It can be overwhelming to take on the entire situation at once. It is important to take things one step at a time and to focus on the present moment. Taking small steps to address the problem can be helpful in managing the situation

5. **Keep perspective**: It can be difficult to maintain perspective when facing adversity. It is important to remember that this situation is not permanent and that it will eventually pass. Keeping this in mind can help you to stay focused on finding solutions and to not get too discouraged.

Chapter 6: Developing Self-Compassion

Self-compassion involves being kind and understanding towards oneself in instances of pain or failure, rather than being harshly self-critical or judgmental. It includes the feelings of kindness, understanding, and acceptance of oneself, regardless of one's perceived shortcomings or mistakes. Self-compassion is an important tool in emotional regulation and resilience, as it allows us to make sense of our emotions and experiences without judgment.

The practice of self-compassion involves three key components: self-kindness, common humanity, and mindfulness. Self-kindness involves treating oneself with kindness and understanding, rather than with harsh criticism or judgment. Common humanity involves recognizing that all humans experience pain and suffering, and that one's own experiences are part of the human experience. Mindfulness involves being aware of our emotions and experiences in the present moment, without judgment.

Self-compassion can be practiced in a variety of ways, including through mindful self-compassion exercises such as mindful breathing, self-compassion mantras, and writing self-compassion letters. Mindful breathing is a simple exercise that involves focusing on one's breath and noticing any thoughts or emotions that arise without judgment. Self-compassion mantras are simple statements of kindness that can be repeated throughout the day. Writing self-compassion letters involves writing a letter to oneself that incorporates self-kindness, common humanity, and mindfulness.

Self-compassion can also be practiced in daily life. For example, when faced with a difficult or challenging situation, it can be helpful to take a step back and adopt a self-compassionate perspective. This might involve recognizing that all humans make mistakes, that we all have moments of pain and suffering, and that it is ok to be imperfect. Additionally, when faced with a setback or failure, it can be helpful to practice self-kindness rather than self-criticism.

Self-compassion can be a powerful tool for emotional regulation and resilience. When practiced regularly, it can help us to be more understanding and accepting of ourselves and our emotions, and to better cope with difficult and challenging situations.

Effects of Self Compassion on the Mental Health

Self-compassion is the process of being kind to oneself, understanding and accepting one's weaknesses and imperfections, and having a sense of understanding and compassion towards oneself. People who practice self-compassion often have a better understanding of their own emotions and are better able to accept their mistakes and weaknesses.

Research has shown that self-compassion has a number of positive effects on mental health. Studies have shown that self-compassion can reduce stress, anxiety, and depression. People with higher levels of self-compassion are better able to cope with difficulties, setbacks, and failures. They are also better able to forgive themselves for their mistakes and accept their flaws. People with higher levels of self-compassion have been found to have higher levels of self-esteem and self-acceptance.

Self-compassion has also been linked to improved physical health. Studies have shown that people with higher levels of self-compassion are more likely to engage in healthy behaviors, such as exercise and healthy eating, and are less likely to engage in unhealthy behaviors, such as smoking and excessive drinking.

In addition, self-compassion has been linked to improved relationships. People who practice self-compassion are more likely to be empathetic and understanding towards others, and are less likely to be judgmental or critical. Self-compassionate people are also better able to accept criticism, take responsibility for their own behaviors, and forgive others.

Overall, self-compassion has a number of positive effects on mental health. By practicing self-compassion, people can become more aware of their own emotions and better able to cope with difficult situations. Self-compassion can also lead to improved physical health, better relationships, and higher self-esteem.

Steps to developing Self-Compassion

1. **Acknowledge Your Feelings**: Recognize and accept your emotions without judgment. Instead of beating yourself up for feeling down, recognize that you are having a difficult time and give yourself permission to feel your emotions.

2. **Practice Self-Kindness**: Speak to yourself in the same way you would to a friend who is having a hard time. Treat yourself with compassion and understanding, rather than with criticism and judgment.

3. **Embrace Your Imperfections**: Everyone makes mistakes and has weaknesses. Instead of focusing on what is wrong with you, focus on what you can do to improve yourself.

4. **Take Time for Yourself**: Make time to do something that you enjoy, such as reading a book or taking a walk. This can help you to relax and recharge.

5. **Challenge Your Negative Thoughts**: When you find yourself thinking negative thoughts, challenge them by asking yourself if the thoughts are realistic and helpful.

6. **Be Gentle with Mistakes**: Instead of beating yourself up when you make a mistake, remind yourself that mistakes are an important part of learning and growth.

7. **Practice Mindfulness**: Mindfulness is the practice of being present and aware of your thoughts, emotions, and environment. Taking time to be mindful can help you become more aware of your thoughts and feelings, allowing you to respond to them with kindness and understanding.

8. **Seek Support**: When you are struggling, reach out to supportive friends and family members or consider seeking professional help.

9. **Celebrate Your Achievements**: It is important to recognize your successes and give yourself credit for your hard work.

10. **Make Self-Care a Priority**: Taking time to care for yourself is essential for your physical and mental wellbeing. Make sure to get enough sleep, eat healthy foods, and engage in activities that bring you joy.

Self-compassion is a powerful tool for improving our mental well-being. It helps us to be kinder and more understanding of ourselves, to accept our failures and shortcomings without judgment, and to keep striving for our goals despite setbacks. Self-compassion can also help us to recognize and accept our positive qualities and accomplishments. It can help us to be more mindful of our thoughts and feelings, and to treat ourselves with respect and care. Ultimately, self-compassion is a skill that can help us to build a strong foundation for our emotional health, allowing us to live with greater peace and joy.

Self-compassion is not about being perfect, it is about accepting ourselves for who we are and taking steps to improve our lives. Practicing self-compassion can help us to be more compassionate and understanding towards others, and to live a life that is more meaningful and fulfilling.

So, if you want to cultivate more peace, joy and contentment in your life, consider practicing self-compassion. It can open the door to a deeper connection with yourself and with life itself.

Part III: Connecting with Others

Connecting with others is an important part of life that can help us form meaningful relationships and build healthier, more fulfilling lives. It allows us to tap into our own inner resources as well as gain insight into the perspectives of others. It can be as simple as having a conversation with a friend or engaging in activities that help us to bond with one another. Whether through social media, face-to-face interactions, or activities such as volunteering or participating in a club, connecting with others can help us develop a sense of belonging and foster a sense of community.

Connecting with others is not always easy, especially in a world where technology can be used to create barriers. However, it is important to make an effort to reach out to those we care about and make time to engage in activities that foster meaningful relationships. It gives us an opportunity to learn more about ourselves and others, to gain insight into different cultures and beliefs, and to understand the world around us from a variety of perspectives.

Connecting with others also helps us to build trust and create lasting relationships, whether those relationships are with family, friends, coworkers, or strangers. It can help us to develop our interpersonal skills, improve our communication, and build our self-confidence.

Overall, connecting with others is an essential part of life that can help us forge strong relationships, build healthy communities, and create meaningful experiences. It can open us up to new experiences, teach us more about the world, and help us to develop a better understanding of those around us.

Making the effort to reach out to those we care about and foster relationships with those around us can be an incredibly rewarding experience. Connecting with others is an important part of life that can help us to grow, learn, and create stronger bonds with those we care about.

So, if you're looking to build stronger relationships, create meaningful experiences, and foster a sense of belonging, start connecting with others today!

Chapter 7: Building Healthy Relationships

What are Relationships?

Relationships are an integral part of life and can provide us with a great deal of joy and love, but they can also be challenging and complex. Relationships can be with family members, romantic partners, friends, colleagues, or anyone else with whom we interact in our lives.

No matter the type of relationship, all relationships require time, effort, trust, and communication in order to be successful. Whether it is a relationship with a partner, family member, or friend, it is important to establish and maintain healthy boundaries, respect each other's opinions, and be willing to compromise.

Communication is key in all relationships. It is important to be honest and open with your partner, and to be willing to listen to their perspective. It is also important to express your needs and wants, and to be able to handle disagreements in a peaceful and mature manner.

Relationships can be immensely rewarding, but they also require a lot of work. It is important to remember that relationships are not perfect, and that conflicts and difficult times are a natural part of any relationship. In order to maintain a healthy relationship, it is important to be patient, understanding, and to be willing to work through any issues that may arise.

Relationships can bring a great deal of joy and love into our lives, but they also require a great deal of dedication and effort. With time, patience, and communication, any relationship can be successful.

These are just some of the many aspects of relationships. It is important to remember that no two relationships are the same, and that each relationship requires its own unique approach. The most important thing in any relationship is to be honest, open, and willing to communicate.

By taking the time to nurture, understand, and invest in our relationships, we can all benefit from the wonderful rewards that relationships bring.

There are many different types of relationships that people experience in their lives. These can range from family relationships, such as parent-child, sibling, or extended family relationships, to romantic relationships between partners, friendships, and even professional relationships. Each type of relationship has its own unique dynamics and characteristics.

Family relationships are some of the strongest and most important relationships that people experience in their lives. Parent-child relationships are the most fundamental and form the basis of all other family relationships. These relationships are based on love and commitment and involve teaching, nurturing, and providing guidance. Sibling relationships involve both positive and negative dynamics such as competition, rivalry, and support. Extended family relationships involve more distant relatives, such as aunts, uncles, and cousins, and are also based on love and commitment, though not necessarily as close as those between parents and children.

Romantic relationships involve a deep emotional connection between two people and typically involve physical intimacy and commitment. These relationships involve trust, communication, and compromise. Friendships are also based on love and commitment, though the nature of the relationship is usually less intense and involves more of a platonic connection. These relationships involve sharing, mutual understanding, and support.

Professional relationships involve interactions between people in a work or business setting. These types of relationships are based on mutual trust and respect and involve cooperation, collaboration, and communication.

No matter the type of relationship, all relationships require effort, patience, and understanding. Relationships can be incredibly rewarding, but also incredibly difficult and complex. It is important to be mindful of the different types of relationships in our lives and to treat each person with respect and care.

The effects of Relationships on the Mental Health

The effects of relationships on mental health can be both positive and negative. Positive relationships can provide individuals with a sense of safety, security, and connection, while negative relationships can be damaging to one's mental health.

Positive relationships can provide individuals with a sense of connection, support, and understanding. Having supportive relationships can be beneficial to mental health as it can provide individuals with a sense of security and comfort. These relationships can be used as a source of support and help individuals cope during times of stress. Additionally, feeling connected to others can help boost self-esteem and feelings of worthiness.

Negative relationships can have an adverse effect on mental health. These relationships can be characterized by constant criticism, judgment, and manipulation. These types of relationships can lead to increased levels of stress, anxiety, and depression. Additionally, negative relationships can lead to decreased self-esteem and feelings of loneliness.

Overall, the effects of relationships on mental health depend on the type of relationship. Positive relationships can be beneficial to mental health, while negative relationships can be damaging. It is important for individuals to recognize the potential effects of relationships on their mental health and take steps to ensure their relationships are healthy and supportive.

Toxic Relationships

Toxic relationships are relationships that are emotionally and mentally damaging. They are characterized by a lack of trust, respect, and communication. Toxic relationships can lead to physical and psychological harm, as well as a sense of insecurity, loneliness, and fear.

Identifying a Toxic Relationship

A toxic relationship is often characterized by one partner attempting to control the other partner's behavior. This can include manipulating the other partner, belittling them, or tearing them down. Other signs of a toxic relationship may include:

- Constant criticism or belittling
- Verbal abuse
- Controlling behavior
- Intimidation or manipulation
- Lack of respect
- Gaslighting

- Isolation from friends and family
- Jealousy or possessiveness

Breaking Free from a Toxic Relationship

Breaking free from a toxic relationship can be difficult, as it often involves confronting the person who is causing the harm. It is important to remember that you cannot control someone else's behavior and it is up to them to make any necessary changes. Here are some steps you can take to break free from a toxic relationship:

- **Recognize the signs**: Understanding the signs of a toxic relationship can help you identify when it is time to leave.
- **Reach out for help**: Talk to a trusted friend or family member about the situation. They can provide valuable insight and support.
- **Set boundaries**: Establishing boundaries can help protect you from further harm.
- **Create a safety plan**: If you are in an unsafe situation, develop a safety plan to help you get out.
- **Seek professional help**: If you need additional help, seek professional counseling or therapy.

• **Practice self-care**: Taking care of yourself is essential in any situation. Make sure you are getting adequate rest, nutrition, and exercise.

Breakups can be difficult, but remember that it is important to take care of yourself and not to stay in an unhealthy relationship. It is possible to break free from a toxic relationship and create a healthier and happier future.

Ten steps to building healthy Relationships

Building healthy relationships is key to having a happy and successful life. It's important to take the time to nurture your relationships, as they can be the source of much joy and fulfillment. Here are some tips on how to build healthy relationships:

1. **Respect**: Respect is the foundation of any healthy relationship. Respect each other's opinions, beliefs, and feelings. Listen to each other's perspectives and be open to compromise.

2. **Communication**: Communication is essential to any relationship. Effective communication involves being honest and open. Listen to each other's point of view and share your own.

3. **Trust**: Trust is an essential part of any healthy relationship. Trust allows for vulnerability and intimacy. Show your trust in your partner by being honest and loyal.

4. **Support**: Support each other in times of need. Offer kind words and encouragement and be there for them.

5. **Compassion**: Show compassion for each other's feelings and experiences. Acknowledge each other's differences and be understanding.

6. **Time**: Spend quality time with each other and make an effort to stay connected. Show your partner that you value them and their time.

7. **Boundaries**: Respect each other's boundaries and learn to compromise. Respect each other's privacy and space.

8. **Gratitude**: Show appreciation for your partner and express your gratitude for their presence in your life.

9. **Forgiveness**: Forgive each other for past mistakes and be willing to move forward.

10. **Fun**: Have fun together and enjoy each other's company. Laugh, share experiences, and make memories.

These are just a few tips to help you build healthy relationships. Remember that relationships take work, but the effort is worth it. With dedication and effort, you can create a lasting and meaningful bond.

Building healthy relationships takes time and effort, but it is worth the work. Showing respect, communication, trust, support, compassion, time, boundaries, and gratitude are all essential components of a healthy relationship. Take the time to nurture your relationships and build a strong foundation of trust and understanding.

With these tips, you can start to build strong and healthy relationships with your family, friends, and significant others.

Chapter 8: Practicing Empathy

What is Empathy?

Empathy is the ability to understand and share the feelings of another. It is an emotional response to someone else's plight, where a person can literally feel what the other person is feeling. It is the capacity to recognize, feel and understand another's emotion and/or experience as if it were one's own, and to respond with appropriate actions and/or words.

Empathy is an important part of being human and is essential in our personal and professional relationships. It is the ability to put yourself in another person's shoes and to experience their feelings as if they were your own. It helps us to build strong relationships and connect with others on a deeper level. It is a powerful tool for creating meaningful connections and understanding others.

Empathy helps us to understand and appreciate differences in opinions, beliefs, and perspectives. It allows us to better understand the world around us and to be more compassionate and supportive. Empathy has been found to improve social relationships, reduce conflict, enhance communication and build trust.

Empathy is a skill that can be developed and strengthened with practice. It requires being aware of our own emotions and being mindful of the emotions of others. We can practice empathy by listening actively and without judgment, really engaging with what the other person is saying and understanding their feelings. It is also important to be open to the feelings of others and to be comfortable with expressing our own feelings.

Empathy is a critical skill in any field or profession, as it helps us to better understand the needs of others. It is particularly important in the fields of health care, education, law, and mental health, where professionals must be able to empathize with their clients, patients, and colleagues.

Empathy is a valuable tool for improving our relationships and building strong connections with others. It allows us to better understand the needs of others and to respond to them with compassion and understanding. By developing and strengthening our empathy skills, we can become better communicators and more understanding and supportive people.

In a nutshell, empathy is an important part of being human and is essential in our personal and professional relationships. It allows us to better understand the feelings of others and to respond with appropriate actions and/or words. Empathy has been found to improve social relationships, reduce conflict, enhance communication and build trust. We can develop and strengthen our empathy skills by listening actively, being open to the feelings of others, and being comfortable with expressing our own feelings.

Developing Empathy in Children

Empathy is the capacity to understand another's feelings and experiences from their perspective. It is an important life skill that can help children become kinder and more compassionate people. Developing empathy in children can help them form strong relationships and improve their social and emotional wellbeing.

1. Model Empathy: Parents and caregivers can help children learn empathy by modeling it themselves. When children see adults showing compassion and understanding to others, they will be more likely to do the same. Give children opportunities to observe you being kind and considerate to others. Show them how to take another person's perspective and ask them questions about how they think the other person might be feeling.

2. Read Books: Reading books with characters who demonstrate empathy can help children understand the concept. Talk about the characters' feelings and choices and how they may have impacted the other characters. Discuss the consequences of the characters' behavior and the impact it had on the outcome of the story.

3. Participate in Service Projects: Participating in service projects with children can help them learn empathy by providing them with an opportunity to help others in need. Working with a charity organization, helping to clean up a local park, or doing something special for a neighbor can all help children learn the importance of helping others.

4. Play Games: Games that involve putting oneself in another's shoes can help children learn empathy. Role-playing games, such as "What Would You Do?", can help children practice making decisions from another person's perspective. Board games and card games that involve cooperation and collaboration can also help children understand the importance of taking turns and considering the feelings of others.

5. Talk About Feelings: Talking about feelings can help children learn to recognize and understand the emotions of others. Ask children open-ended questions to encourage them to think about how their actions may affect someone else's feelings. Use stories and examples to help them understand how their behavior may have an impact on another person.

Developing empathy in children is an important life skill that can help them build strong relationships and become better communicators. By modeling empathy and talking about emotions, playing games, reading stories, and participating in service projects, parents and caregivers can help children learn empathy and become more compassionate people.

Developing Empathy in Adults

Empathy is an important part of being a functioning adult. It allows us to better understand and relate to others, and foster meaningful connections. Developing empathy takes time and effort, but it is worth the effort. Here are some tips for developing empathy in adults:

1. Listen actively. Listening actively means engaging with the speaker and paying attention to nonverbal cues. Listen without judgement and try to understand the other person's perspective.

2. Put yourself in their shoes. When someone is sharing their experience, try to imagine what it would be like to be in their position. This can help to deepen your understanding of the situation and what the other person is feeling.

3. Practice self-awareness. Empathy starts with understanding ourselves. Take time to reflect on how your own experiences shape your understanding of the world and how it affects how you relate to others.

4. Be open to learning. Be open to learning about others' experiences, even if they are different from your own. This will help you to develop a more compassionate understanding of the world.

5. Show kindness. Showing kindness to others can help to foster empathy. Simple acts of kindness such as a smile or lending a helping to hand can go a long way.

6. Take responsibility for your own feelings. Taking responsibility for your own feelings will help you to better understand and empathize with other people's feelings.

By taking the time to practice these tips, adults can develop empathy and foster meaningful connections with others. Empathy is an important part of being a functioning adult, and it can lead to a more fulfilling and connected life.

Overall, empathy is a key component of being an empathetic adult. It is important to take the time to develop this skill and practice it in your daily interactions. With practice, you can become a better listener, become more understanding of others, and foster meaningful connections.

Empathy in our everyday lives

Empathy plays an important role in everyday life, as it helps us to understand other people's feelings and perspectives, and to be more compassionate and caring towards them. Empathy is the ability to understand, share, and respond to another person's feelings, thoughts, and experiences – without judgment.

One example of empathy in everyday life is when a friend is having a hard time and you take the time to listen to them and show them your support and understanding. You might put yourself in their shoes and try to imagine how you would feel in their situation. By showing genuine empathy and compassion, you can provide a comforting and supportive environment for your friend.

Another example of empathy in everyday life is when you are interacting with strangers. For example, if you are in a store and the cashier is having a bad day, you can take the time to show them empathy and understanding. You might take the time to ask them how they are doing and offer a few kind words of encouragement. By showing empathy and understanding to a stranger, you can make their day a bit brighter.

Also, empathy in everyday life also plays a role in parenting. When a child is having difficulty understanding a concept or is feeling overwhelmed, it is important for a parent to show empathy and understanding. By empathizing with the child and helping them to feel seen and understood, a parent can provide the child with the emotional support they need to get through the situation.

Empathy is an important skill to have in everyday life. It helps us to understand and connect with others in a meaningful way and to be more compassionate and supportive towards them. By showing empathy and understanding in our everyday interactions, we can make the world a better place for everyone.

The Benefits of Practicing Empathy

1. Improved Relationships: Practicing empathy leads to better relationships with friends, family, and coworkers. It helps people to understand each other better and build stronger, healthier bonds.

2. Increased Understanding: Being able to see things from someone else's perspective allows us to better understand their feelings, thoughts, and behaviors.

3. Improved Communication: Empathy helps us to communicate more effectively and build better relationships. It helps us to better understand what someone else is trying to say and how they are feeling.

4. Stress Relief: Practicing empathy can reduce stress levels, as it helps us to be more understanding and patient with others.

5. Conflict Resolution: Empathy can help to resolve conflicts by allowing us to step into the other person's shoes and understand their point of view.

6. Better Decisions: Being able to think from someone else's perspective can help us make better decisions. It increases our understanding of what is best for the situation and how to handle it.

7. Increased Compassion: Practicing empathy can help us to be more compassionate and understanding towards others. It can help us to be more accepting and tolerant of people who are different from us.

Empathy, like we have discussed is the ability to understand and share the feelings of another. This is an invaluable skill that can benefit both individuals and society. Practicing empathy can lead to greater understanding, compassion, and connection between people. It can also help to reduce conflict and create positive relationships.

At the individual level, practicing empathy can help to create a sense of self-awareness. By understanding the emotions and experiences of others, we can better understand our own feelings and emotions. We can become more in tune with our own thoughts and feelings, which can lead to more meaningful relationships and more satisfying lives.

Practicing empathy can also help to foster better relationships. When we understand and appreciate the feelings of others, we are better able to connect with them. This can lead to more meaningful conversations, mutual understanding, and deeper connections. Empathy can help to bridge the communication gap between people, even those of different backgrounds and perspectives.

Empathy can also benefit society as a whole. When we empathize with others, we can gain a better understanding of their perspectives and experiences. This can help to reduce prejudice and discrimination, as well as lead to greater acceptance and understanding of others.

Overall, practicing empathy can be beneficial in many areas of life. It can help us to build better relationships, understand people better, communicate more effectively, and make better decisions.

Chapter 9: Cultivating Kindness

What is Kindness?

Kindness is a quality that is often underrated, yet it is one of the most powerful tools we have in our arsenal. It is an act of compassion and consideration that can be expressed in many ways and can have a profound impact on those who receive it. Kindness can be expressed through giving, helping, sharing, listening, and encouraging. It can be a simple smile, a kind word, or a hug. It can be offering a helping hand, going out of your way to help someone, or showing someone that you care.

The power of kindness is far-reaching and can benefit both the giver and the receiver. For the giver, acts of kindness can help to foster an environment of connection, compassion, and understanding. It can help to reduce stress, increase happiness and create a sense of purpose. For the receiver, kindness can bring comfort, hope, and joy. It can help to build self-esteem, reduce feelings of isolation, and create a sense of belonging.

In today's society, we are often busy with our own lives and needs, and it can be easy to forget that our words and actions can have a profound impact on others. Practicing kindness can help to remind us of our interconnectedness and can help us to show care, compassion, and respect for those around us. It can help to build relationships, foster empathy, and create a more positive and inclusive world.

In times of crisis and difficulty, kindness can be a powerful source of comfort and hope. It can help to reduce fear and anxiety, provide support, and create a sense of unity. Kindness can be expressed in many ways, from donating time or money to a charitable cause, to simply offering a kind word or gesture.

No matter how small the act, kindness can make a difference. Kindness can enrich our lives, build relationships, and create a more positive and connected world. It is a powerful tool that can help us to foster understanding and compassion, and to create a more peaceful and just society.

Therefore, the next time you have the opportunity, express kindness and watch the ripple effect it has on those around you.

The Benefits of Being Kind

Being kind is one of the greatest gifts one can give to oneself and to others. Being kind brings a range of benefits, both to the giver and the receiver.

Being kind helps to build relationships and create a sense of community. When we are kind to one another, it creates a feeling of connection and belonging. It shows others that we care and that we are interested in their wellbeing. Kindness is contagious and can help to create an atmosphere of positivity and acceptance in a group.

Being kind can also help to build self-confidence and lead to more positive self-esteem. When we do something kind for others, we can feel a sense of pride, knowing that we have done something good. This can help us to feel more self-worth, which can in turn help us to feel happier and more secure.

Being kind can also help to reduce stress. Kindness releases oxytocin, a hormone that helps to reduce stress and anxiety. It can also help to reduce cortisol levels, which is linked to increased stress, as well as improve our overall mental health.

Finally, being kind can help to improve our physical health. Kindness can help to reduce inflammation, which can help to reduce the risk of illnesses such as heart disease. It can also improve the immune system and help to reduce blood pressure.

Being kind is a simple yet powerful act that can bring about so many benefits. It can help to create a sense of connection and belonging, build self-confidence and self-esteem, reduce stress, and improve our physical health. It is an act of love that can make a difference not only in our own lives, but in the lives of those around us.

So be kind. You'll be glad you are.

Kindness in the Workplace

Workplace kindness is a concept that is often overlooked in favor of focusing on efficiency and productivity. However, fostering a culture of kindness in the workplace can have a great impact on job satisfaction, morale, and overall productivity.

When employers and employees alike make an effort to be kind and supportive of one another, it creates an atmosphere of trust and openness in the workplace. This, in turn, encourages collaboration and cooperation, and boosts morale and productivity. Kindness in the workplace is also beneficial to employee wellbeing, as it improves workplace relationships and reduces stress.

There are many ways to cultivate a culture of kindness in the workplace. Managers should strive to create a supportive work environment and treat all employees with respect and dignity. They should provide support and recognition for employees' efforts, show appreciation for a job well done, and demonstrate empathy for their employees.

Employees should also take the initiative to be kind and supportive of their co-workers. This could include offering help and assistance, providing feedback and constructive criticism, or simply taking the time to get to know each other.

Also, it is important to recognize that kindness is a two-way street. Employers should be open to feedback from their employees and strive to create an environment where people feel safe to express their opinions and ideas. This will help foster an atmosphere of mutual trust and respect, and ensure that everyone feels valued and appreciated.

In truth, kindness in the workplace is an important and often overlooked aspect of running an effective and successful business. It can improve job satisfaction, morale, and overall productivity, and create an atmosphere of trust and openness in the workplace. Taking the time to be kind and supportive of each other is an important part of fostering a positive and productive work environment.

To sum it up, workplace kindness is an essential part of any successful business. It fosters a culture of trust and respect and encourages collaboration and cooperation among employees, resulting in a more productive and satisfying work environment. Employers and employees alike should strive to be kind and supportive of each other, and take the time to get to know each other in order to create an atmosphere of mutual trust and respect.

Workplace kindness has a positive impact on an individual's mental health. Kindness in the workplace can reduce stress, improve morale, and create a more positive work environment.

Workplace stress is a major source of mental health issues. A kind workplace can help combat this by providing more support and understanding. Having kind coworkers and supervisors who are willing to listen and provide constructive feedback can help reduce the stress of a demanding job. Kindness can also help build a sense of community, making the workplace more enjoyable and creating a more positive environment.

Morale is also improved when kindness is present in the workplace. Kindness creates a sense of trust and respect between coworkers, which can lead to better collaboration and team building. A kind workplace also encourages openness and honesty between coworkers, making it easier to address issues and resolve conflicts.

Finally, having a kind workplace can make it easier to feel connected to the job. Kindness in the workplace can help create a sense of belonging, making it easier to stay motivated and engaged with the job. This can lead to better job satisfaction and improved mental health.

Overall, workplace kindness has a positive effect on an individual's mental health. A kind workplace can reduce stress, improve morale, and create a more positive work environment. This can help create a healthier and more productive work environment for everyone.

The Power of Kindness in Relationships

Kindness is a powerful force in relationships. It can be the glue that binds two people together, or the spark that ignites a flame of love. It can be a source of comfort and security, or a source of strength and courage.

When kindness is present in a relationship, it can help to foster trust, understanding, and mutual respect. Kindness can bring out the best in people, helping them to be more open, honest, and vulnerable with each other. It can help to create a safe space in which both parties can be vulnerable and share their feelings.

Kindness can also help to build self-confidence and self-esteem. When a person feels appreciated and valued, it can be a great source of comfort and self-worth. It can also help to create a more positive outlook on life, as well as a greater sense of purpose and meaning.

In addition to these positive effects, kindness can also help to strengthen relationships. It can help to bring people closer together, by making them feel connected and appreciated. Kindness is a great way to show someone that you care and that you value them. It can also be a great way to show gratitude and appreciation.

Finally, kindness can help to create a sense of security and safety. When someone feels safe, they are more likely to be open and honest with each other. This can lead to deeper conversation, greater understanding, and a stronger connection between two people.

Overall, the power of kindness in relationships is undeniable. It can be a source of comfort, security, and strength. It can also help to foster trust, understanding, and mutual respect. Ultimately, it can be a powerful force for good in any relationship.

No matter what kind of relationship you are in, kindness is always a great thing to keep in mind. It can make a world of difference in any relationship, and help to create a stronger bond between two people.

So next time you're in a relationship, remember to show kindness to your partner. It can make a huge difference in your relationship, helping to create a stronger bond and a more positive outlook on life.

Practicing Kindness in Everyday Life

Practicing kindness in everyday life is an important part of creating a meaningful, harmonious existence. We can all make a conscious effort to be kinder to ourselves and to those around us. Kindness can take many forms, from the simplest of gestures to more meaningful acts of service. Regardless of how it is expressed, kindness can have a significant impact on both the giver and the recipient.

The first step to practicing kindness in everyday life is to treat oneself with kindness. Self-care is an essential component of being kind to oneself. It involves taking time to relax and do something that brings joy and fulfillment. This could be anything from reading a good book, taking a walk, or spending time with loved ones. Self-care also involves setting boundaries and taking care of one's physical and mental health.

The second step to practicing kindness in everyday life is to express kindness to others. This can be as simple as smiling or saying hello to someone in passing. It can also take the form of holding the door open for someone, offering to help with a task, or sending a thoughtful gift. Kindness towards others can also come in the form of volunteering or helping out in the community.

No matter how small or insignificant it may seem, kindness can have a huge impact. It can make someone's day or even change their outlook on life. It can also have a ripple effect, inspiring others to be kind as well. Practicing kindness in everyday life is a great way to spread love and positivity and create a better future for everyone.

In conclusion, practicing kindness in everyday life is an essential part of creating a meaningful, harmonious existence. It involves treating oneself with kindness, as well as expressing kindness to others. Kindness can take many forms, from the simplest of gestures to more meaningful acts of service. No matter how small or insignificant it may seem, kindness can have a huge impact on both the giver and the recipient. For these reasons, it is important that we all make a conscious effort to be kinder each day.

Part IV: Unlocking Joy

Unlocking joy is the intentional exploration of how to experience joy in life. It is an exploration of how to create joy on a consistent basis. It is an exploration of how to find and develop the tools necessary to unlock joy in our lives.

The first step in unlocking joy is to recognize that joy is a choice. We have the power to choose to be joyful or not. We have the power to choose to focus on the negative or focus on the positive. We have the power to choose how we respond to the events of our lives. We have the power to choose to be present and enjoy the moment or to ruminate on the past and worry about the future.

The second step in unlocking joy is to cultivate an attitude of gratitude. It is easy to become overwhelmed and consumed by negative emotions, but it is important to make an effort to recognize the good in life. No matter how small, take a moment to recognize and be thankful for the good things in life. Being thankful and grateful helps us to find joy even in the most difficult circumstances.

The third step in unlocking joy is to cultivate positive relationships. Being around positive people can help to lift our spirits and increase our joy. Spending time with those who we can trust and who build us up helps to foster an environment where joy can flourish.

The fourth step in unlocking joy is to practice self-care. It is important to take care of ourselves physically, mentally, and emotionally. Eating a healthy diet, getting enough sleep, and engaging in regular physical activity are all important components of self-care. Additionally, it is important to take time to relax and enjoy life. This could be taking a walk in nature, reading a book, writing in a journal, or engaging in any activity that brings us joy.

The fifth step in unlocking joy is to recognize our worth. It is important to recognize that we are worthy of joy and to be kind to ourselves. We are all imperfect and it is important to recognize and accept our imperfections. It is important to recognize that we are worthy of joy and to make an effort to practice self-love.

Unlocking joy is a journey. It is an exploration of how to create joy on a consistent basis and how to find and develop the tools necessary to unlock joy in our lives. With intention, practice, and patience, we can unlock joy.

In this final part, we will be discussing some topics and we will see how the recommendations from these topics can help us unending joy.

Chapter 10: Exploring the Benefits of Mindfulness for Achieving Lasting Joy

Mindfulness is a powerful tool for achieving lasting joy. It is a practice of cultivating awareness and acceptance of the present moment. Mindfulness helps us to be present, to be aware of our thoughts, feelings, and body sensations without judgment. It teaches us to be more aware of our actions and reactions, and helps us to respond more skillfully to difficult situations.

By practicing mindfulness, we can learn to be more aware of our thoughts, feelings, and body sensations. This can help us to become more aware of our internal state, allowing us to better manage our thoughts and emotions. When we are able to be more aware of our feelings and thoughts, we can respond to them in a healthier and more mindful way. We can practice self-compassion, allowing us to move through difficult emotions and experiences with greater ease.

Mindfulness can also help us to become more aware of our environment and the people around us. We can become more aware of how our behavior impacts the people around us, as well as more aware of how our environment affects our mood. This can help us to make better decisions about how to interact with our environment, as well as how to manage our stress levels.

Mindfulness can help us to cultivate greater self-awareness, leading to greater self-acceptance and self-love. When we are able to accept ourselves for who we are, we can be more present in our lives and appreciate the beauty and joy that exists in each moment. We can also become more aware of our needs and desires, allowing us to better take care of ourselves and create a life that is fulfilling and meaningful.

Finally, mindfulness can help us to cultivate greater resilience. When we are able to be mindful of our thoughts, feelings, and body sensations in difficult situations, we can respond more skillfully and remain in control of our emotions. This can help us to become more resilient to stress and difficult situations, allowing us to move through life with greater ease and grace.

Overall, mindfulness can be a powerful tool for achieving lasting joy. By cultivating greater awareness and acceptance of our thoughts, feelings, and body sensations, we can learn to be more present in our lives and appreciate the beauty and joy that exists in each moment. We can also become more aware of our environment and the people around us, allowing us to make better decisions about how to interact with our environment and manage our stress levels. And finally, we can cultivate greater resilience and be more mindful of our thoughts, feelings, and body in difficult situations, allowing us to move through life with greater ease and grace.

By practicing mindfulness regularly, we can learn to be more present in our lives and cultivate lasting joy.

Examining the Effects of Mindfulness on Mental and Emotional Well-Being

Mindfulness is a popular term that is often used to describe a state of awareness and focus on the present moment. It involves paying attention to one's thoughts, feelings, and physical sensations in an effort to become more aware of how one is feeling in the present moment. Mindfulness has been increasingly studied in recent years as a way to improve mental and emotional well-being. Research has shown that mindfulness-based interventions can reduce symptoms of depression, anxiety, and stress, as well as improve overall psychological functioning and quality of life.

The basic idea behind mindfulness is that by being aware of the present moment and the feelings associated with it, it is possible to become more in tune with oneself and one's environment. This increased awareness can help an individual to better understand their thoughts and feelings, allowing them to make more effective decisions and choose healthier behaviors. Mindfulness has also been associated with improved concentration, as well as better decision-making and problem-solving skills.

Mindfulness is often practiced through meditative and contemplative activities, such as yoga, tai chi, and qigong. These activities can help to reduce stress and promote relaxation. Mindfulness meditation specifically involves focusing on the breath, allowing thoughts and feelings to come and go without judgement or analysis. This type of meditation can help to reduce rumination and worry, while also improving concentration and focus.

In addition to its effects on mental and emotional well-being, mindfulness has been associated with numerous physical health benefits. Studies have found that mindfulness can improve immune system functioning and reduce inflammation. It can also help to reduce pain, improve sleep quality, and reduce blood pressure.

Overall, mindfulness can be a powerful tool for improving mental and emotional well-being. It can help to reduce stress and anxiety, while also improving concentration and focus. Additionally, mindfulness can have numerous physical health benefits, such as improved immune system functioning and reduced inflammation. Therefore, it is an important tool for anyone looking to improve their overall health and well-being.

Understanding the Role of Mindfulness in Stress Reduction and Self-Care Practices

Mindfulness is an increasingly popular technique for reducing stress and promoting self-care. Mindfulness is a state of being in which one is aware of the present moment without judgment. It is a practice of non-judgmental awareness that allows one to observe their thoughts, feelings, and sensations without being attached to them. Through mindfulness, individuals become aware of their thoughts, feelings, and bodily sensations in order to gain insight into their own behavior, attitudes, and beliefs.

Mindfulness-based approaches to stress reduction and self-care focus on developing the capacity to pay attention to the present moment, to be non-judgmental, and to cultivate a sense of acceptance and self-compassion. By being mindful, individuals can become aware of their thoughts and feelings and recognize the physical sensations associated with stress. This awareness helps individuals to develop skills that can be used to respond to stress in a mindful and compassionate manner.

Mindfulness can help individuals recognize and accept their distress and reduce their reactivity to it. Through the practice of mindfulness, individuals can gain insight into how their thoughts and feelings affect their behavior. This awareness can help individuals develop healthier behavior patterns and increase their sense of self-control. Additionally, mindfulness can help individuals become more aware of the impact of their stress on their body and physical health, enabling them to take steps to address it.

Mindfulness-based approaches to stress reduction and self-care also focus on self-care practices, such as self-reflection, relaxation, and physical activity. Self-reflection helps individuals to become aware of their thoughts and feelings and to identify their sources of distress. Relaxation techniques, such as yoga and meditation, can help individuals to reduce the physical symptoms of stress and to promote a sense of calmness. Physical activity can help to reduce stress levels, boost mood, and improve overall health.

Also, mindfulness-based approaches to stress reduction and self-care can help individuals to cultivate a sense of self-compassion and acceptance. Through self-compassion and acceptance, individuals can learn to be kinder to themselves and to accept their mistakes and imperfections. This can help to reduce feelings of stress and anxiety, and improve overall well-being.

Overall, mindfulness-based approaches to stress reduction and self-care can help individuals to develop the capacity to pay attention to the present moment, to be non-judgmental, and to cultivate a sense of acceptance and self-compassion. Through this practice, individuals can become more aware of their thoughts and feelings and develop healthier behavior patterns. Additionally, mindfulness can help individuals to become more aware of the physical symptoms of stress and to take steps to address it. Finally, mindfulness-based approaches to stress reduction and self-care can help individuals to cultivate a sense of self-compassion and acceptance, which can reduce feelings of stress and anxiety and improve overall well-being.

Investigating the Benefits of Mindfulness in Enhancing Connection and Meaningful Relationships

Mindfulness is a concept that has been gaining popularity in recent years. It is defined as a mental state achieved by focusing one's awareness on the present moment, while calmly acknowledging and accepting one's feelings, thoughts, and bodily sensations. It has been studied extensively, and researchers have found that it can have a positive impact on physical and mental health as well as relationships. In particular, there is evidence to suggest that mindfulness can enhance connection and meaningful relationships.

One of the most obvious ways in which mindfulness can improve relationships is by increasing self-awareness. When people are more mindful and aware of their own thoughts, feelings, and reactions, they can better understand those of others and respond in a more caring way. This can lead to more meaningful conversations and deeper connections with others. Additionally, mindfulness can help people to be more present in their interactions with others, which can create a more positive atmosphere.

Mindfulness also helps individuals to be more accepting of themselves and others. It encourages people to look beyond their own biases and accept the thoughts and feelings of others without judgement. This can lead to more open and honest communication, which is essential for fostering meaningful relationships. Additionally, mindfulness can help individuals to be more patient and understanding, which can build trust and strengthen relationships.

Finally, mindfulness can help individuals to become more mindful of their own emotions, which can lead to greater self-compassion. This can lead to more authentic relationships, as individuals can be more open and honest about their feelings and experiences. Furthermore, self-compassion can help people to better manage their emotions, which can lead to more positive and productive conversations.

Overall, the evidence suggests that mindfulness can have a positive impact on relationships. By increasing self-awareness, acceptance, and self-compassion, individuals can build stronger and more meaningful connections with others. It is an important skill to cultivate, as it can help people to better understand and communicate with one another, fostering deeper and more meaningful relationships.

Chapter 11: Connecting with Nature for Greater Contentment

Exploring the Benefits of Nature for Mental Health

Mental health is an important topic that is receiving increasing attention in today's society. Mental health disorders, such as depression and anxiety, are on the rise, creating a need for new approaches to mental health care. One of the most promising new approaches is the use of nature for mental health. Exploring the benefits of nature for mental health can help individuals to better manage their mental health and can provide a more holistic approach to mental health care.

The use of nature for mental health is not a new concept. For centuries, people have been using natural elements such as sunlight, plants, and water to promote healing and relaxation. In recent years, however, research has shown that nature can have a positive impact on mental health. Studies have shown that spending time in nature can reduce stress and anxiety levels, improve mood, and even reduce symptoms of depression. Additionally, exposure to natural elements can increase creativity and productivity, as well as improve memory and focus.

There are many ways to use nature for mental health. One of the most popular approaches is to spend time outside in green spaces. This can include walking or running in the park, gardening, or simply taking time to sit and observe nature. Research has also shown that spending time in nature can improve physical health, which can also have a positive effect on mental health. Other activities such as yoga and meditation in nature can help to reduce stress and anxiety levels and promote relaxation.

The benefits of nature for mental health are clear, but there are also some potential risks that should be considered. For example, spending too much time outdoors can lead to sunburn, insect bites, and other physical health issues. Additionally, some people may find the vastness of nature to be overwhelming, which can lead to feelings of isolation. It is important to find the right balance and to be aware of one's own needs when exploring nature for mental health.

Exploring the benefits of nature for mental health is an important step in creating a more holistic approach to mental health care. By incorporating nature into mental health care, individuals can reduce stress and anxiety levels, improve mood, and improve overall physical and mental well-being. Nature can be an effective, natural way to promote healing and relaxation, and more research is needed to understand the full potential of nature for mental health.

Here are 10 benefits of nature to the mental health:

1. Stress Reduction: Being in nature can help reduce stress and anxiety by providing a calming environment to take a break from the hustle and bustle of everyday life.

2. Improved Mood: Spending time in nature can help improve mood and reduce depression.

3. Increased Attention Span: Research has found that spending time in nature can help improve attention span, particularly in children.

4. Improved Cognitive Function: Studies have found that being in nature can help improve cognitive function, such as memory, decision-making and problem-solving.

5. Better Sleep: Nature can help promote better sleep by providing a calming environment, free of distractions.

6. Increased Physical Activity: Spending time in nature encourages physical activity, which can help improve overall physical and mental health.

7. Improved Social Interaction: Being in nature can provide an opportunity to connect with others and engage in meaningful conversations.

8. Increased Self-Awareness: Spending time in nature can help increase self-awareness and promote mindfulness.

9. Boosted Immune System: Research has found that spending time in nature can help boost the immune system and reduce inflammation.

10. Reduced Blood Pressure: Being in nature can help reduce blood pressure and improve cardiovascular health.

Finding Balance Through Nature-Based Activities

Nature-based activities are a great way to promote balance in our lives. By connecting with nature, we can find a sense of peace and well-being. Nature-based activities can provide us with an opportunity to escape our busy lives and find a sense of balance.

Nature-based activities can help us to reconnect with ourselves and the environment. By engaging in activities such as hiking, camping, or bird-watching, we can take a break from our hectic schedules and focus on the present moment. Taking a break from the technology and digital world can help us to reconnect with ourselves and the environment.

Nature-based activities can also be beneficial for our physical and mental health. By engaging in activities such as yoga, Tai Chi, or walking in nature, we can reduce stress and anxiety. Exercise can also help to improve physical health, and nature-based activities can provide a calming and enjoyable way to get some exercise.

Finally, nature-based activities are an excellent way to foster a sense of community. By engaging in outdoor activities with friends and family, we can build relationships and promote a sense of belonging. This can help us to feel more connected to our community and to the environment.

Nature-based activities are a great way to promote balance in our lives. By engaging in activities such as hiking, camping, or bird-watching, we can take a break from our hectic schedules and find a sense of peace and well-being. Nature-based activities can also provide us with an opportunity to exercise, reduce stress and anxiety, and foster a sense of community. By connecting with nature, we can find a sense of balance in our lives.

Cultivating a Sense of Gratitude for Nature

Cultivating a sense of gratitude for nature is a key part of living a balanced and healthy life. This can be done through taking time to appreciate and experience nature, connecting with nature through activities such as gardening and hiking, and by developing a sense of respect for nature's resources.

One way to cultivate a sense of gratitude for nature is to take the time to appreciate and experience nature. This can be done by simply taking a walk in a nearby park or by visiting a local natural area. Taking a few moments to observe the beauty of nature can be a powerful experience.

Taking a pause to appreciate the sights and sounds of nature can help to foster a sense of appreciation and gratitude.

Another way to cultivate a sense of gratitude for nature is to connect with it through activities such as gardening and hiking. Gardening can provide an opportunity to develop a connection with the earth and to appreciate the beauty of nature. Hiking can be a great way to get out into nature and to appreciate the natural beauty of the area.

Finally, developing a sense of respect for nature's resources is another way to cultivate a sense of gratitude for nature. Taking the time to learn about and understand the importance of protecting nature can help to foster a sense of respect for the environment and its resources. This might include understanding the importance of sustainable practices and conserving natural resources.

Cultivating a sense of gratitude for nature is an important part of living a balanced and healthy life. Taking the time to appreciate and experience nature, connecting with nature through activities such as gardening and hiking, and by developing a sense of respect for nature's resources can all help to foster a sense of appreciation and gratitude for the environment.

This appreciation of nature is important because it can help to foster a sense of connection to the environment and help to inspire us to protect and conserve nature. Cultivating a sense of gratitude for nature can help to foster a sense of respect for the environment and its resources and can help to inspire us to take action to protect the environment.

Connecting to Nature for Stress Relief

Connecting to nature is an age-old practice that has been known to provide numerous health benefits, including stress relief. The practice of reconnecting with nature has recently become more popular as people have begun to look for healthier and more holistic ways to manage stress. Nature provides an environment that is free from the hustle and bustle of everyday life, allowing us to unwind and relax. Studies have shown that spending time in nature can reduce stress, improve mood, and even improve overall physical health.

One of the most beneficial activities for stress relief is to take a walk in nature. Taking a walk in a park or forest is a great way to get away from the stresses of everyday life and reconnect with nature. Walking allows us to observe the beauty of nature, appreciate its vibrant colors and sounds, and take in its calming atmosphere. Walking in nature is also an effective way to clear your mind and become more mindful of your surroundings.

Another effective way to connect with nature for stress relief is to simply sit in a natural area for a period of time and do nothing. This practice is known as 'forest bathing' and is becoming increasingly popular as a way to relax and restore balance. Sitting in a natural area and simply being present allows us to become more aware of our surroundings, be mindful of our thoughts, and practice being in the moment. This type of activity can be incredibly calming and can help to reduce stress, improve mood, and encourage feelings of peace and wellbeing.

Finally, another great way to connect with nature and reduce stress is to practice yoga or meditation outdoors. Practicing yoga or meditation outside allows us to be fully present in the natural environment, taking in its sights, sounds, and smells. Outdoor yoga and meditation can be incredibly calming, allowing us to reconnect with nature, improve our physical and mental wellbeing, and reduce stress.

Overall, connecting with nature is an effective and holistic way to reduce stress and improve overall wellbeing. Taking a walk in nature, forest bathing, and practicing yoga or meditation outdoors are all effective ways to relax and reconnect with nature. Nature provides us with an environment free from the hustle and bustle of everyday life, allowing us to unwind, relax, and reduce stress.

If you're looking for a healthier and more holistic way to reduce stress, connecting to nature is a great option. Taking some time to reconnect with nature can be incredibly calming and beneficial for your mental and physical health.

Chapter 12: Developing Optimism for Increased Well-Being

Optimistic Thinking Strategies

Optimistic thinking strategies are ways of looking at the world and our lives in a positive light. They can help us to focus on the good things in life and to be more resilient in the face of adversity. Optimistic thinking can help us to be more successful, have better relationships, and to have a healthier outlook on life. Here are some strategies for becoming a more optimistic thinker:

1. **Acknowledge Your Strengths and Accomplishments:** It's easy to forget all the good things we have done in our lives, but it's important to take a moment to recognize our accomplishments and appreciate our strengths. This can help to boost our self-confidence and give us a more positive outlook.

2. **Practice Positive Self-Talk**: Our thoughts have a huge influence on how we feel and the decisions we make. It's important to be mindful of the words we use to talk to ourselves and make sure they're positive and affirming.

3. Reframe Your Thoughts: It's easy to get stuck in negative thinking patterns and to assume the worst. When this happens, it's important to challenge our thoughts and look for the silver lining. Taking a moment to reframe our thoughts can help us to gain a more optimistic point of view.

4. Take Time to Be Grateful: Gratitude is a powerful tool for shifting our focus to the good things in life. Taking a few moments each day to reflect on what we're thankful for can help us to cultivate an attitude of optimism.

5. Connect with Others: Connecting with other people is a great way to get outside of our own heads and to remember that we're not alone. Taking time to reach out to friends and family, or to volunteer in the community, can help to put our own struggles in perspective and to gain a more positive outlook.

By practicing these strategies, we can learn to be more optimistic thinkers and find more joy and contentment in life.

Establishing an Optimistic Mindset

Optimism is critical to our success in life. It helps us see the bright side of things, even when the odds are not in our favor. Having an optimistic mindset can be the difference between staying stuck in a rut and making progress. It can be the difference between feeling overwhelmed and feeling empowered. It can be the difference between giving up and taking action.

Establishing an optimistic mindset requires setting specific goals and working toward them. It requires understanding that setbacks are part of the process and that failure is not the end, but rather an opportunity to learn and grow. It requires a commitment to be positive, even when things are not going as planned. It requires a willingness to take risks and try new things, even if they seem scary.

It is also important to surround yourself with positive people who can help keep you motivated. Surrounding yourself with like-minded people is key to staying focused on your goals and remaining optimistic in the face of adversity.

Finally, it is important to take care of yourself. Get enough sleep, eat healthy, exercise, and practice self-care. Taking care of your body and mind will help you stay focused and have the energy to pursue your goals.

By following these steps, you can establish an optimistic mindset and start seeing the world in a brighter light. With an optimistic mindset, you can start believing in yourself and achieve the success you desire.

Practicing Positive Self-Talk

Positive self-talk is an essential tool of self-care, and an important part of mental health. It is the practice of speaking kindly to yourself, using statements that focus on the positive, rather than the negative. It can help you to overcome negative self-talk, and to cultivate a more positive outlook on life.

Positive self-talk can help to increase your self-esteem, as it encourages you to focus on your strengths and abilities. It can also help to reduce stress, by allowing you to focus on positive aspects of a situation rather than the negative. Additionally, positive self-talk can help to increase motivation, by reinforcing the idea that you are capable of achieving your goals.

The practice of positive self-talk begins with becoming aware of how you talk to yourself. Start by paying attention to the words that you use when thinking or speaking to yourself. Are they positive or negative? Are they encouraging or discouraging? If they are negative, make an effort to replace them with positive statements.

It can also be helpful to identify triggers for negative self-talk, and to develop strategies for responding in a positive way. For example, if you tend to feel down when you make a mistake, recognize this as a trigger and remind yourself that mistakes are part of learning.

In addition to replacing negative statements with positive ones, it can also be helpful to write down positive affirmations and to recite them daily. These affirmations can be tailored to your own needs, and can provide a source of motivation in challenging times.

Finally, it is important to practice positive self-talk consistently. It can be helpful to set aside a few minutes each day to focus on positive affirmations and self-reflection. With practice, positive self-talk can become an effective tool in helping to cultivate a more positive outlook on life.

Leveraging Positive Social Support Networks

Social support networks are defined as the network of social relationships that provide emotional and tangible support to an individual. Positive social support networks are often characterized as those which are supportive, encouraging, and provide a high level of emotional support. Leveraging positive social support networks is an important skill for individuals to master, as it can have a profound impact on one's overall mental and emotional health.

Positive social support networks can provide individuals with a sense of belonging, which can help to reduce feelings of loneliness and isolation. Additionally, these networks can provide emotional and practical support during times of difficulty, such as during periods of illness, bereavement, or other life transitions. In some cases, individuals may even look to their positive social support networks for advice and guidance.

In order to effectively leverage positive social support networks, individuals should first identify who is in their network and what type of support they can provide. It is important to recognize that support networks can be comprised of family members, friends, colleagues, and even online acquaintances. Individuals should also be aware of their own personal needs and how they can be supported by others in their network.

Once individuals have identified the members of their positive social support networks, they should then reach out and actively engage with them in meaningful ways. This could include having regular phone conversations or video calls, setting up virtual coffee dates, or participating in virtual activities together. Additionally, individuals should make sure to express appreciation and gratitude to their support network members for their ongoing support.

Finally, individuals should strive to maintain their positive social support networks by actively cultivating and nurturing their relationships. This could include sending birthday cards, scheduling regular check-ins, or sending encouraging messages. By engaging in these activities, individuals can ensure that their positive social support networks are strong and can provide them with the emotional and practical support they need.

Conclusion

In conclusion, The Joy of Living: A Guide to Lasting Happiness is a book that provides readers with the tools to help them live happily and to find peace and contentment within themselves. Through the book, readers have been able to learn that true happiness comes from living in the present moment and embracing the joy that comes with it. Furthermore, readers have been given insight into the spiritual aspects of life and the importance of connecting with one's inner self in order to find lasting happiness.

The book also encourages readers to be mindful of their thoughts, feelings, and actions and to take responsibility for all of them. By doing so, readers are able to create a positive attitude and outlook on life that allows them to move forward even when things are not going the way they had hoped. Finally, readers have learned that lasting happiness comes from having a life that is filled with meaningful relationships, meaningful experiences, and finding purpose and meaning in life.

Overall, The Joy of Living: A Guide to Lasting Happiness provides readers with the tools and insight needed to find true and lasting happiness. By following the advice and guidance of the book, readers can move forward in life with a positive attitude and outlook, creating a life filled with joy, contentment, and peace.

The Joy of Living: A Guide to Lasting Happiness is a book that provides readers with the knowledge and understanding needed to find true and lasting happiness. Through the book, readers have been given insight into the spiritual aspects of life and how to create a life filled with joy, contentment, and peace. The book encourages readers to be mindful of their thoughts, feelings, and actions and to take responsibility for them. The book also provides readers with the tools needed to find meaningful relationships and experiences, as well as finding purpose and meaning in life. Through the words of this book, readers have been given the tools needed to find true and lasting happiness in their life.

In conclusion, The Joy of Living: A Guide to Lasting Happiness is an incredibly valuable book that provides readers with the tools and insight needed to create a life filled with joy and peace. This book is a must-read for anyone looking to find true and lasting happiness in their life.

www.ingramcontent.com/pod-product-compliance
Lightning Source LLC
LaVergne TN
LVHW050318160826
845677LV00014B/3455

* 9 7 9 8 3 7 0 7 7 9 4 0 4 *